ONE DAY ORIGAMI
MASTERY

The Complete Beginner's Guide to Learn Origami in Under 1 Day!

15 Step by Step Projects That Inspire You– Images Included

By Ellen Warren

2

Note from the Author:

Did you know that you can make a beautiful crane out of one single sheet of paper without using glue? That's what's amazing about origami, the art of paper folding. By following a pattern of folds, you can create incredibly beautiful paper sculptures.

At the beginning of this book, you will start with a simple sheet of paper. You will then fold your way through simple folds. As you do, you will familiarize yourself with their names and shapes. Moving from there, you will create traditional origami bases. After that, you will make simple origami models. Then finally, you will end up making more challenging origami sculptures.

This book contains proven steps and strategies on how to become a truly great origami artist. Learn how to make the Boat, Fish, Crane and the Horse. These are a few of the many origami figures that you will learn to make simply by folding paper in a particular pattern. Detailed instructions are provided inside each chapter.

What makes origami so great is its versatility. As an art form, origami is not limited in its form or function. There are many different patterns for creating the same figure. You can choose a simple pattern or a more elaborate pattern depending on your skill level or tastes. You can use a simple color paper or an intricate design. You can even use plain white copy paper. You can even experiment and make the same model using different papers until you find the one that looks best to you.

Life does get hectic, but creating an origami figure doesn't take long. Origami provides you with a quick break that allows you to relax and refocus. As you practice your origami skills, your imagination will spring into action. You'll start to envision other shapes that you can make from different combinations of folds. You'll start to see origami shapes in objects around you. Let this creative insight inspire you to create your own patterns. The only limit to your origami collection is your own creative imagination.

Ellen Warren

Chapter Index

The Basics

Are you looking for a hobby that is fun and easy to learn? Are you wanting to learn how to make your own decorations? Or, are you simply looking for a way to relax? Origami can be the way to answer yes to all of these questions.

What is Origami?

Origami is the art of folding paper to create a work of art. The word comes from Japanese, *ori* means "folding" and *kami* means "paper". How simple is that? Origami is based on simple principles and simple foundational folds, when combined, that can create complicated structures. While the term origami comes from Japan, paper folding existed in China long before it did Japan. People have been practicing paper folding for around 2,000 years. Origami is an ancient practice that is still relevant today. Paper folding serves several different functions.

Uses for Origami

Origami has long been used to create decorations. You can make centerpieces for tables at a party. You can decorate gift packages with origami shapes. You can make a string of origami wedding dresses to decorate for a bridal shower. The uses for origami-based decorations are only limited by your imagination.

Another use for origami is education. Paper folding offers children so many valuable lessons. First of all, origami improves hand-eye coordination. It's excellent for developing fine motor skills, and this is why origami has been used in teaching students with disabilities. Secondly, origami teaches sequencing and following instructions. If you don't follow the instructions exactly, your paper sculpture won't turn out right. In addition to these lessons, origami also teaches you how to focus and gain a sharper attention to detail. If you don't focus on what you're doing, the duck you're trying to make might end up looking like a dragon. Finally, origami teaches patience. You can't rush through the steps and expect a beautiful creation. You have to take your time when first learning a new shape. Even after you've mastered a shape, you still need to take your time because mistakes stand out in origami. Origami is a practice in beauty, and this can't be rushed.

Not only does origami serve decorative and educational purposes, but paper folding can be therapeutic, as well. The amount of focus that required to successfully turn a piece of par crane helps you take your mind off of your troubles. The patience needed to make intricate folds helps you relax. Overall, practicing origami has a calming effect.

If these reasons weren't enough to convince you to try origami, then the greatest reason of all will: it's fun! Origami was practiced by the Imperial Court of Japan over 1,000 years ago as a way of passing the time, and it's still used the same way today. You can create origami shapes while sitting at home. You can practice origami while waiting for a meeting to start (I might suggest that, while origami can help you make it through a boring meeting, you might not want to make a giraffe during a meeting and upset your boss!).

Simply origami is a great hobby to learn. You get all of these great benefits, and at little cost. With origami, you're not going to have the costs of other hobbies such as model airplane building. This is because the materials you need to create artistic shapes out of paper are minimal.

What You Need for Origami

The basic tools you use in origami are your hands. That's what makes origami great. You don't have to buy specific tools for the hobby. There's no glue or paint to buy. You don't have to use special cutting tools. Instead, you use the basic tools you were born with: your hands.

Other than your hands, you need paper. That's it. Origami is nothing more than folding paper with your hands in a series of steps to create a shape. The cost of origami is much cheaper than scrapbooking. You're not going to run into the same costs with origami as you would collecting stamps or coins because paper is highly available and relatively cheap (unless you want a specific design, but even then it's still not costly). You can buy a 500 count package of origami paper that contains multiple colors for under $20. That's 500 paper sculptures for under $20.

Origami Paper
Kami, traditional origami paper, is thin so that it can be folded easily. It's also weighted enough to hold a crease, but not too heavy that you can't eliminate a crease if you make a mistake. It's usually colored on side and white on the other. *Kami* comes in many different sizes, but a common size that is sold is a 6 in. square.

In addition to *kami*, foil-backed paper can be used if you want to make a design that is intricate and requires the paper to hold its fold. Foil-backed paper is a thin sheet of aluminum foil that is glued to a thin sheet of paper. Some origami enthusiasts like using foil-backed paper to practice intricate fold patterns because of its ability to hold a crease well. This ability can also be a problem if using foil-backed paper at other times because it's unforgiving: once you a mistake, the mistake will show more than with other paper types.

You Could Use Other Tools If You Needed To
Origami is such a versatile hobby. If you don't have any *kami* near you, you can always use copy paper. You'd simply have to cut the 8 ½ in. x 11 in. copy paper into a square. You'd need a pair of scissors.

As for making different size sculptures, you can purchase different sizes of origami paper. Or, you can buy a larger size, say a 10 in. square and cut a piece down to the size you want. If you do this, you'll have more origami paper to use. Also, you don't have to just buy squares. Origami paper also comes in other shapes, like a circle, for sculptures that require such shapes. Again, you can always cut these shapes out of a square piece of paper. In these cases, you would need scissors, ruler, pair of compasses, and a pencil to mark where to cut.

Another tool that is used by some origami practitioners is a bone folder. A bone folder is used to mark and crease paper. Originally bone folders were made from animal bones, thus the name. Today, bone folders are made from plastic, as well.

Now that you know the basics of origami and you see how useful and efficient origami is as a hobby, you're probably itching to get your hands on a piece of paper and begin folding. Enthusiasm is good. It'll help you appreciate the art of origami more, and will make your origami experience more enjoyable. If you're ready to learn origami, the place to begin is with some standard fold techniques, but before you take these on it might be helpful to know some tips for great looking origami.

Some Tips <u>Before</u> You Begin

As you've seen already, origami can be a fun hobby to learn. Yet, origami is more than a hobby. It's an art form. Truthfully, it will take time to learn how to fold the paper properly to create beautiful paper sculptures. Anything creative takes effort, but the results can be astounding. If you want astounding origami figures, there are a few tips that can help you.

Take Your Time

Origami is a practice in patience. Don't rush through the folds. Take the time to make each fold correctly. If you don't take your time to correctly execute each step, your figure will not look right in the end. More than that, origami is supposed to be relaxing. You can't relax if you're rushing through the steps. If you want origami to stay enjoyable, take your time. Enjoy the process.

Go For Accuracy

More than being a practice in patience, origami is a practice in accuracy. Review the diagrams. Follow the instructions exactly as they are given. Make precision folds. Be sure that edges match up when folding. Be precise. The beauty of origami is sharp lines and symmetry. Lacking accuracy in your folding destroys this beauty. Start with soft creases. If you make a mistake, correcting the mistake will be easier with a soft crease. With a soft crease, the evidence of a mistake will not be as evident, if it's evident at all. Once you've made the fold and it's accurate, make the crease again using a hard crease.

Work in a Clean Area

This includes having clean hands before you start. You don't want dirty hands to ruin the paper. Also, if you're using a flat surface on which to fold, make sure it's clean, as well. Again, you don't want stains on your completed figure.

Learn as Much as You Can

Don't settle for knowing a few simple patterns. Increase your repertoire. Work your way through various levels of difficulty. Start with simple patterns and work up to difficult patterns. Read up on origami on the internet. Watch instructional videos. Experiment with the process. Create your own designs. Get the most out of origami. It's your hobby. More than that, it's your craft. It's your art form.

Practice

Origami, like any art that requires skill, needs to be practiced. The old saying, "practice makes perfect", holds true for origami. The more you practice folding, the better you will get at it. Practicing folding helps you to remember the steps. It also helps you remember the positions of the folds, as well. More than anything, by consistently folding, you'll reap all of the benefits of origami that were mentioned previously.

Don't Give Up

When you make a mistake, and you will, don't give up. Simply try again. You may be able to save the paper from a mistake, or you may have to use a new piece of paper. That's why you should always fold a new pattern on cheaper paper, in case you have to start over on a new piece of paper. You may want to attempt to patterns on copy paper, so that you won't waste *kami*. Also, you may want to work through a new design with a larger piece of paper. This will help you complete the folds completely. Once you mastered the new design, you can then move to a smaller, more expensive piece of paper.

Show Off Your Paper Sculptures

Find some way to exhibit your creations. Take a picture of them to share on social media. Keep a photo album. Display them somewhere in your house. Decorate your office with your origami sculptures. Use your origami artwork to decorate for special events. Give them away as gifts. Join an online origami forum where you can discuss origami and share your creations. Host an origami party where your friends can gather to origami together. Let others enjoy your newly learned talent.

Without Further Ado

Now that all of the basics of origami have been discussed, it's time to get down to the nitty-gritty. The following chapters will take you through your first fold all the way to difficult patterns. By practicing the instructions provided in the remainder of this book, you'll have learned 10 origami designs. That's a strong beginning that you can build upon as you practice your new hobby.

Basic Folds

Since origami has been around for thousands of years, some basic origami techniques have developed. These include basic folds that have traditional names. Knowing these basic folds will help you create origami shapes, since these shapes are made from specific combinations of these folds. You will make these basic folds as individual steps within the patterns you will learn in the chapters that come to follow, so you will need to know what they are called and how to create the fold. So, let's start folding.

Valley Fold

This fold is the most basic fold that you will make in origami. In the Valley Fold, you fold the paper in front of itself, bringing one edge of the paper to align with the opposite edge. Doing so will create a crease in the center of the paper. Or, you could fold the edge of the paper to align to another crease you've created. This action will create a crease in one of the quarters of the page. This fold is called the Valley Fold because, if you hold the sheet with the fold at the bottom, it resembles a valley. For some origami shapes, you'll need to fold and unfold a valley fold. This is called pre-creasing. The valley fold looks like this:

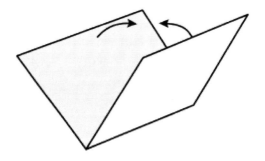

Basic Folds Are an Art Form By Themselves

The valley fold, along with the other basic fold mentioned below, comprises the basis of origami. Some origami patterns only make use of only these basic folds. They are called Pureland Folds and were designed by John Smith in the 1970s. These forms are ideal for beginners and for individuals with disabilities. Smith also believed that a return to the simplicity of the art of origami was needed to preserve the beauty of the art. In any case, Pureland provides an excellent starting point in origami by its reliance on only using the valley and mountain fold.

Mountain Fold
The mountain fold is the exact opposite of the

valley fold. One edge of the paper is folded behind another. The crease will be on top. Like the valley fold, the mountain fold can be horizontal, vertical, or diagonal. The folded paper looks like a mountain as you can see here:

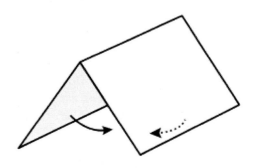

("Mountain Fold" by Fred the Oyster, CC By 3.0.)

The Reverse Fold

In addition to the valley and mountain folds, another fold frequently used in origami is the reverse fold. It's often used to create the heads and tails of animal models. There are two types of reverse folds: the inside reverse fold and the outside reverse fold.

Inside Reverse Fold

The inside reverse fold is always applied to a corner flap that is created either by a valley or mountain fold. Essentially, this fold reveals the inside of the corner flap to the outside, as you can

20

see in the image below.

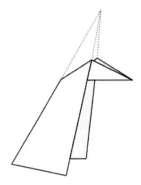

To make an inside reverse fold:

1. Make a valley fold where you want make the inside reverse fold.
2. Unfold.
3. Push the top corner in between the two layers of the paper.
4. Reinforce the creases by pressing firmly.

Outside Reverse Fold

The outside reverse fold allows the paper to change directions. It is commonly used in the feet of animal models. It's also used to make the heads of certain bird models. Instead of the fold being positioned in between the layers of the paper, like in an inside reverse fold, the outside reverse fold allows the paper to cover back over itself.

21

To make an outside reverse fold:

1. Make a valley fold where you want to place the outside reverse fold.
2. Unfold.
3. Peel the layers of the paper away and fold at the crease line.
4. Reinforce the folds by pressing firmly.

The outside reverse fold looks like this:

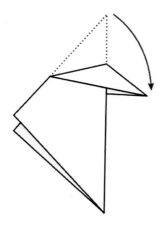

("Outside Reverse Fold" by Fred the Oyster, CC-By-3.0.)

Pleat Fold

The pleat fold can be thought of using several different metaphors: a fan, an accordion, or stair steps. This fold is basically comprised of alternating valley and mountain folds.

To make a pleat fold:

1. Make a valley fold.
2. Make a mountain fold where the bottom layer of paper ends (where the valley ends).
3. Continue the process for however many pleats you need.

A pleat fold looks like this:

The Blintz Fold

The blintz fold is made by bringing the folding the four corners of the paper to the center. You use this fold when making a pinwheel. The image below details what the blintz fold looks like.

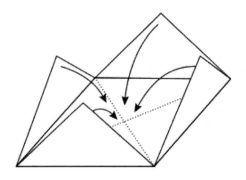

("Blintz Fold" by Fred the Oyster, CC-BY-3.0.)

To make the blintz fold:

1. Valley fold and unfold the paper left to right.
2. Valley fold and unfold the paper top to bottom.
3. Valley fold the corners toward the center. Start with any corner and then move to corner diagonal from that one. Then, fold the other two.

Squash Fold

The squash fold is used to put a portion of your paper into a position that makes it read for the next fold. Along with other folds, it's important to place the squash fold in the right position. If you don't, the remainder of your folds will be out of alignment, and your sculpture will not look right.

To make a squash fold:

1. Valley fold and unfold flap to be squashed to pre-crease.
2. Lift flap to be squashed toward you (open up the flap.)
3. Pry apart the layers of paper.
4. Change the valley fold to a mountain fold.
5. Press down to squash the paper into place.

The squash fold looks like this:

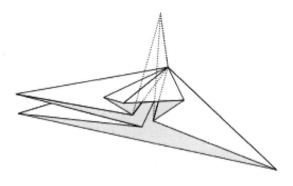

("Squash Fold" by Fred the Oyster, CC-BY-3.0.)

The Petal Fold

The petal fold is used in bird models and in making several flower sculptures. The petal fold is a little more intricate than the other folds, but with enough practice the petal fold will become second nature to you.

To make a petal fold:

1. Valley fold the bottom-left and bottom-right edges to the vertical mid-line.

2. Valley fold the top point down.
3. Unfold the 3 flaps back to step "a".
4. Lift the top-layer of the model up allowing it to collapse along the creases made above.
5. The valley fold made in step a will become a mountain fold.

If done properly, your petal fold should look like this:

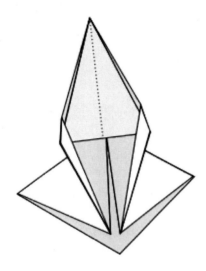

("Petal Fold" by Heron2, CC-BY-3.0.)

The Rabbit Ear Fold
This fold is a combination of three valley folds and

one mountain fold. It's called the rabbit fold because the flap it makes looks like a small rabbit ear.

To make the rabbit ear fold:

1. Make a valley fold in the center of the paper to create a center line and unfold.
2. Make a valley fold with the left side of the top layer toward the center line creating a smaller triangle and unfold.
3. Do the same with the right side and unfold.
4. Re-fold both sides of Steps 2 and 3 at the same time.
5. Form a new flap with the extra paper.
6. Fold the flap to one side.

When done correctly, your rabbit ear fold will look like this:

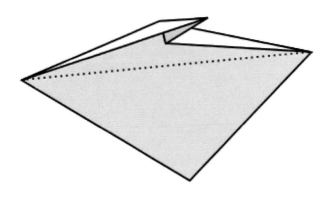

Combining These Basic Folds

The previously discussed folds are only a small handful of the folds that are used in origami, yet they are the most common folds used in origami. By combining these forms, you can create some fundamental bases from which origami sculptures are made. At first, you might struggle through these basic folds. Keep practicing. Eventually you'll complete these folds with ease, so that you can create the fundamental bases of origami. These fundamental bases will be discussed in the next chapter.

Fundamental Origami Bases

Because origami is based upon a pattern, some of the early steps can be combined. When combined, these steps create a base from which to design and create origami models. Several forms may use the same foundational base. The base has the basic geometric shape of the figure you're trying to create. By manipulating the base with further folds according to a pattern, you create the model you want to make. By learning these bases, you can exponentially expand the number of sculptures that you can create. You simply change the steps after you have made the base. Memorizing these forms makes participating in origami easier. Once you've mastered these bases, you can move into creating complete figures. As with folds, the bases progress from simple to difficult.

Shawl Fold

Even though the shawl is called a fold, it is the base for many origami figures. It's a very simple base, and is one of the traditional ancient Japanese bases. It's also called a triangle fold because that's the shape the paper takes when the fold is completed.

To make a shawl fold:

1. Turn the sheet of paper so that a corner is at the top. Your paper will look like a diamond, instead of a square.
2. Valley fold the paper in half. You should now have a triangle.
3. Press the fold to crease it.

Square Base

Another base that is fundamental to many origami patterns is the square base. Just like the shawl fold, the square base is aptly named because of its shape. The square base is also called the preliminary fold because other bases are built upon this base. Another name for the square base is the flower base because several origami flowers are based upon it.

To make a square base:

1. Make a shawl fold.
2. Make a valley fold from left to right, making a smaller triangle.
3. Make a squash fold.

The steps for completing the square base look like:

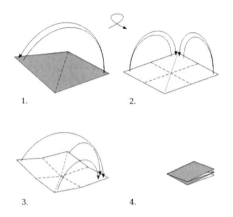

Water Bomb Base

The water bomb base is the inverted form of the square base. This traditional name comes from ancient Japan where these origami bases were actually used to make an origami models that were used as the predecessor to the water balloon. For this reason, it's also called the balloon base.

To make a water bomb base:

1. Make pre-creases using two valley folds (one right to left and the other top to bottom) with the color side facing up (if using *kami*).
2. Make an X pre- crease by first making a diagonal valley fold from top left corner to bottom right corner. Unfold and make

31

another diagonal valley fold from top right corner to bottom left corner.

3. Fold top of edge of the paper down while squeezing the side edges.

The steps for completing the water bomb base look like:

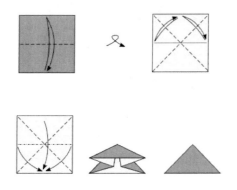

The Kite Base

The kite base is named because it looks like a kite when it's completed. The kite base is the starting point for making a whale or a swan. This base is very simple to make. It basically consists of three valley folds with the paper shaped like a diamond.

To make a kite base:

1. With the paper white side facing up and shaped like a diamond, make a valley fold from left to right creating a triangle. Press the crease and unfold.
2. Fold the bottom left and right sides to the center crease.

The steps for making the kite base look like:

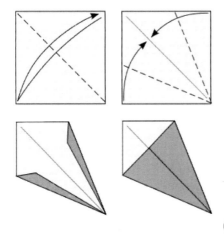

The Bird Base

This base is pretty self- explanatory as to why it's called the bird base. It's the base that is used to make the traditional crane figure that most people associate with origami. Again, the bird base is

33

simple in that it's a square base followed by two petal folds.

To make a bird base:

1. Make a square base.
2. Turn the square base to look like a diamond.
3. Valley fold the lower edges of the front flaps to the center crease.
4. Crease and unfold.
5. Valley fold the top down so that the top of the square bas is now flat.
6. Crease and unfold.
7. Pull front flap up so that sides are connecting.
8. Squash fold down.
9. Crease.
10. Turn over the base.
11. Repeat Steps 7-9.

The steps for completing the bird base look like:

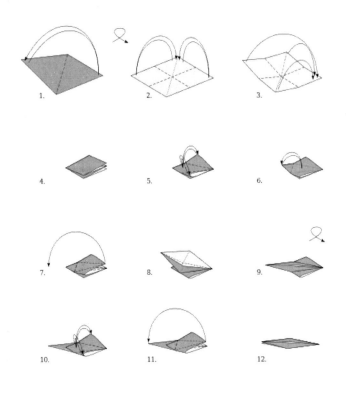

The Fish Base

Along with being used to start an origami fish, the fish base is also used to start an origami cat. The fish base is made from two kite bases and is diamond shaped.

To make the fish base:

35

1. Start with paper colored side down and in diamond shape.
2. Make one shawl fold bringing top right corner down to bottom left corner.
3. Crease and unfold.
4. Make another shawl fold going the opposite direction (top left to bottom right corner).
5. Make a kite base.
6. Make another kite base, but this one is an upside down kite.
7. Pinch the left and right sides and collapse to center along diagonal pre-creases.
8. Close the flaps up.

The Helmet Base

The helmet base looks like a samurai helmet. It can either be a figure in itself or used as a base. It's the base for an easy goldfish.

To make a helmet base:

1. With color side down and paper shaped like a diamond, make horizontal valley fold to create a triangle.

2. Crease.

3. Valley fold left corner to bottom corner.

4. Valley fold right corner to bottom corner. You should now have a smaller diamond.

36

5. Valley fold top two corners outward slightly.

6. Valley fold bottom toward top, but don't go all the way to the top.

7. Valley fold top layer slightly to create an extra strip at the center of the base.

The steps for creating the helmet base look like:

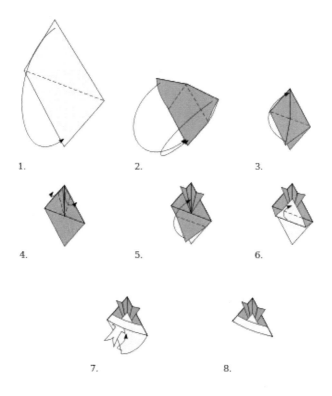

The frog base

In addition to being the base of the origami frog, the frog base is also the foundation for the iris. This base is a little more advanced than the other bases and takes a little more time to make. Once you've mastered it, though, you'll be able to create one in a shorter amount of time.

To make the frog base:

1. Make a square base.
2. Bring one of the flaps up so it's perpendicular to the rest of the base.
3. Squash fold this flap.
4. Repeat steps 2 and 3 for the remaining flaps.
5. Petal fold left and right edges.
6. Open up top flap and lift up while pinching its sides until sides meet at center. A triangle shaped flap should be formed.
7. Valley fold triangle flap down.
8. Repeat process for remaining flaps.

The steps for creating the frog base look like:

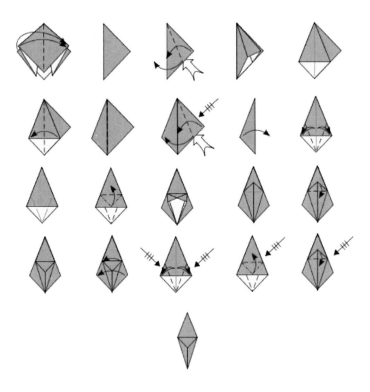

Continue Building From Here

You should practice making these bases until you are confident enough to make them without having to follow instructions. Remember to be accurate. A little mistake in a base will show up as a major mistake in your completed origami model. Continue to use the same tips that you used in learning to make basic folds. Origami is all about the process. As you progress through process, keep your level of focus and patient consistent. By doing so, you will master the bases, just as you have mastered the traditional folds. Once you feel confident in your ability to make bases, you are ready to move on to complete origami sculptures.

Easy Origami Figures

Now that you're ready to begin creating actual origami figures, it's important to remember to follow the directions. Each step builds on each other. Make your folds crisp and sharp. Origami is about the lines and the shapes. This chapter begins with some easy origami models that do not require bases. Chapter 6 will include more easy origami models with Chapter 7 introducing origami figures that are a little more intricate.

You should practice each shape until you've memorized the process. This practice will help you finalize the form. Just as you only moved on to the bases after perfecting the traditional folds, you shouldn't move from one model until you've perfected it. This will help you keep the forms separate in your head. Remember, origami can't be rushed. If it's rushed, the final figure will look disfigured.

With that being said, let's look at some easy origami figures. These are not the only easy origami figures by far. They are only a representative sample.

The Jumping Frog

To begin working with easy origami figures, the

first figure to be discussed is the jumping frog. This frog is easy because it simply requires mountain and valley folds. This simple design is included to give you more practice with folding, and to give you a fun, creative model. This frog actually jumps if you press down and release on the back!

To make the jumping frog:

1. Make a horizontal valley fold. Unfold.

2. Fold upper right corner to left edge using mountain fold. Unfold.

3. Fold upper left corner to right edge using mountain fold. Unfold.

4. Make mountain fold to backside where the diagonal creases meet in center.

5. Pinch sides and bring toward center crease. A triangle should form.

6. Fold bottom corners of triangle to meet top point with valley folds.

7. Fold sides toward center crease with valley folds.

8. Make a valley fold with bottom edge meeting where crease lines connect.

9. Fold same part with mountain fold. Bottom edge of paper should meet center crease.

10. Turn over. Jumping frog is complete.

The steps to make the jumping frog look like this:

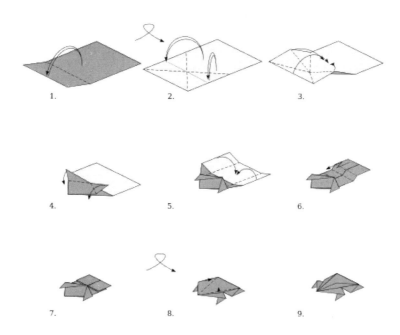

Boat
You'll have lots of fun with this model! You can

make it, and set it off down the water. All you need is paper and some water, and you can pretend to be a sailor. Of course, you'll have to use heavier paper if you want to float this boat. This model uses a rectangular piece of paper, instead of a square one. You can start by making the boat from a regular 8.5 x 11 in. piece of copy paper. Once you've nailed the pattern, you can make boats of all sizes. You can make a whole fleet if you want!

To make a boat:

1. Start with a rectangular sheet of paper. You'll want to have the color side facing up if you use colored paper. Make a horizontal valley fold. Unfold.

2. Make a mountain fold. Crease.

3. Mountain fold corners to center pre-crease. Crease.

4. Valley fold a 2 in. strip of bottom edge of both layers. Crease.

5. Pull on sides and flatten into a square.

6. Turning the square to form a diamond, valley fold front layer bottom tip to meet front layer top tip. Do the same to the back layer. This will form a triangle.

44

7. Pull on sides and flatten into a diamond.

8. Pull on top tips to make boat shape.

9. Flatten to firmly crease. Slightly open sides to create the boat, and you're done.

The steps to making the boat look like this:

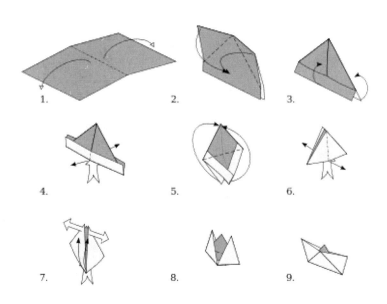

Box

The traditional origami box has many uses. The traditional box is based on the *sanbo*, a Japanese offering container. In keeping with the tradition of offering, you can use the origami box as a candy dish or a gift box. You can use holiday themed paper and make them for Valentine's Day, Christmas, or even St. Patrick's Day. You could put green candy in a box made from green paper. The uses of the origami box are as endless as your imagination.

To make the box:

1. Using a rectangle sheet of paper, color side up, pre-crease the paper by making a horizontal valley fold and unfold. Then, make a vertical mountain fold and unfold. This will make a cross in the center of the paper.

2. Turn the paper over and valley fold the corners to the center of the pre-crease, making a diamond. Unfold. This will pre-crease an X that has the same center as the cross.

3. Push in the side edges causing the top half to collapse on top of the bottom half. The paper will look like you're making a paper airplane.

4. Valley fold the edges to meet at the center pre-

46

crease. Unfold.

5. Valley fold the top layer back to the center again. Crease.

6. Do the same for the back layer.

7. Valley fold ¼ of the bottom half of the front layer to the middle of the paper. Crease.

8. Do the same to the bottom half of the back layer.

9. Turn the paper over, grab the front and back layers on opposite corners, and pull apart while pushing down. The paper will flatten out into its final shape, and the box is complete.

The steps to making the box look like this:

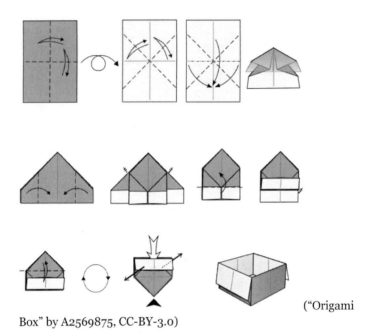

Windmill

The windmill, or pinwheel, is another fun shape to make. You can attach it to a stick to make a pinwheel. Blow on it and watch it spin. This is a great craft for children. It's a little lengthier step-wise, but the steps are pretty simple.

To make the windmill:

1. Using a rectangular piece of paper, horizontally valley fold square piece of paper. Unfold to pre-crease.

2. Valley fold side edges of paper to meet center pre-crease.

3. Diagonally mountain fold top left corner to center pre-crease. Diagonally mountain fold bottom right corner to center pre-crease.

4. Unfold.

5. Turn paper 90 degrees.

6. Diagonally mountain fold top right corner to center pre-crease. Diagonally mountain fold bottom left corner to center pre-crease. Unfold.

7. Unfold valley folds to return to flat sheet of paper.

8. Refold 1st valley fold from top edge. This should be the first ¼ of the top part of the paper.

9. Refold 1st valley fold from left side edge while pushing in the 1st diagonal crease from the left side edge at the top. This should create the first blade of the windmill.

10. Refold 1st valley fold from the bottom edge while pushing in the 1st diagonal crease from the left side edge at the bottom. This should create the second blade of the windmill with the right side looking like a paper folded in half vertically.

49

11. Diagonally mountain fold the two upper layers on the right side while simultaneously pushing on the bottom layer. This will make the third blade.

12. Diagonally mountain refold top right corner along pre-crease line creating the final blade.

13. Crease all folds. The windmill is now complete.

The steps in making the windmill will look like this:

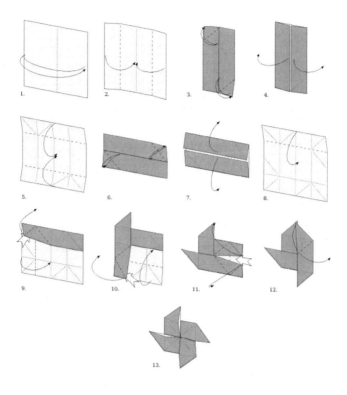

Now that you have finally mastered a few easy origami models, it's now time to take it one step further. In the next chapter, you will learn some easier origami shapes. But this time, there will be no diagrams. Try to complete the steps simply by following the written instructions. Try to visualize what each step looks like. This will help you get better at making origami sculptures.

More Easy Origami Shapes

As you have learned from completing the patterns found in the previous chapters, origami takes time to perfect. It's an art form that needs to be practiced. You won't always get it right the first time. It's better to start out slowly with easy patterns, and then advance to more complicated patterns. You have to walk before you crawl. So, in this chapter, you will learn some additional easy origami patterns. However, the aid of the visual aids has been removed.

When learning these origami models, work on your ability to follow instructions. Create a mental picture of what is to be accomplished. This strengthens your creative abilities.

Once again, you'll start with something simple. The difficulty level will increase as you progress to the next figure. Let's begin with the fox head.

Fox Head

This simple origami figure is simple, yet elegant with its sharp lines. You can leave it unadorned, or you can draw eyes and color in the nose.

To make the fox head:

1. Start with paper color side down in diamond shape.

2. Mountain fold bottom point to meet top point. Crease.

3. Create a pre-crease by making horizontal valley fold to fold triangle in half. Unfold.

4. Mountain fold top half down to meet bottom edge.

5. Valley fold right edge to meet center crease. Crease.

6. Do the same for left edge. Paper should look like a diamond.

7. Flip the paper over to complete.

Fish

One of the more popular origami figures is the fish. One of the joys of origami is that you can make the sculpture as simple or difficult as you want to make it. This fish exemplifies how simple origami can be, while still holding to the traditional appreciation for crisp lines and use of geometric shapes.

To make the fish:

1. Starting with color side down in diamond shape, make a mountain fold to form a triangle. Crease.

2. Valley fold top layer in half. Crease.

3. Valley fold bottom half of bottom layer to meet middle. Crease.

4. On the bottom half of the bottom layer, make a mountain fold a little above the bottom edge leaving a strip on the bottom edge. Crease.

5. Valley fold the left corner back onto paper. Corner should now be sticking up.

6. Mountain fold top of left corner down on top of lower half of left corner.

7. Diagonally mountain fold right corner down over the right edge of the paper.

8. Turn figure over. The fish is now complete.

The Crab

Keeping with the sea theme, let's now move on to the crab. If you're having an ocean themed party, you could decorate using the combination of the fish, the crab, and one more sea creature that you will learn next.

To make the crab:

1. With color side down, vertically valley fold in half. Crease.

2. Make a horizontal valley fold. Your paper should now look like a smaller square.

3. Squash fold top layer. Remember a squash fold is where you open top layer and flatten to create a triangle. Your paper should now look like an upside down triangle overlapping a square.

4. Turn your paper over. Triangle should now be on the left.

5. Squash fold top layer. Your paper should now look like an upside down triangle.

6. Diagonally valley fold ¼ of each edge inward.

7. Turn over. Paper should now look like an upside down triangle with antenna sticking up.

8. Valley fold bottom point upward to leave a straight bottom edge. Crease.

9. Mountain fold down left and right corners.

10. Turn over and done.

The Whale

This whale figure actually uses a kite base. It also rounds out the ocean theme.

1. Make a kite base.

2. Turn kite on its side.

3. Valley fold in left corner (top of the kite on its side) toward middle leaving a straight edge. Crease.

4. Mountain fold kite in half.

5. While pushing down on right corner, flip the corner upward. This makes the tail and completes the whale.

The Lady Bug

Let's turn our attention from the sea to the ground. This lady bug is cute and simple. You can either buy red paper with black spots, or you can use plain red paper and put the spots on yourself with a pen.

To make the lady bug:

1. Start with paper in the shape of diamond with the white side up. Fold paper in half vertically with a mountain fold. This makes an upside down triangle. Crease.

2. Make a horizontal valley fold and unfold to pre-crease.

3. Mountain fold down left and right corners to not quite the center pre-crease leaving a little space in between. Crease.

4. Turn over.

5. Mountain fold top corner to the middle.

6. Make a pleat fold. Remember that a pleat fold is a valley fold that follows a mountain fold with a little space in between the two folds. Crease.

7. Turn model over. The lady bug is then complete.

The Hat

One final figure that can be quite useful is the hat. By learning this origami figure, you can make your own party hats. You can also play Peter Pan or Robin Hood.

To make the hat:

1. Using a rectangular sheet of paper, make a horizontal valley fold to fold the paper in half. Unfold. You now have a center pre-crease.

2. Make a mountain fold to fold the paper in half. Crease.

3. Mountain fold the top corners to the center pre-crease. Crease.

4. Valley fold bottom edge of top layer to the bottom of the triangle. Crease.

5. Valley fold bottom edge again over the bottom of the triangle. Crease.

6. Turn over model and repeat Steps 4 and 5.

7. Open out hat. Shape it and wear because your hat is now complete.

Now that you've completed the hat, you now know 10 easy origami figures. You've learned some figures that you can decorate with. You've learned some figures that you can wear. You've made some figures that make easy toys. Overall, you've put basic origami folding to practice and have strengthened your paper folding skills. Now, it's time to try a few sculptures that are a little more intricate.

A Few Intricate Origami Models

By the time that you've reached this chapter, you have put in the time and effort to practice your paper folding craft. You've advanced from basic folds to easy figures. You know how to properly crease the paper. You've practiced enough that you feel confident with your origami. Now, you're ready for a few origami patterns that are a little more intricate. You're now ready to make origami sculptures using the bases you learned in Chapter 3.

The Crane

The crane is probably the most recognized origami structure. It's a traditional origami figure and symbolizes the art of origami. Most often, when people think of origami they are picturing the crane in their heads. Once you've mastered the crane, you may want to make some cranes using beautifully designed paper. In Japanese culture, the crane is a symbol of good luck. You'll certainly be fortunate to have this model to show off your origami artistry.

To make the crane:

1. Make a bird base.

2. On the top layer, valley fold the edges toward

the center crease. Crease.

3. Turn the paper over and do the same to the back layer.

4. Valley fold bottom points to the top point. Unfold.

5. Diagonally valley fold bottom points back onto to body aligning with it with the edge of the paper. Crease.

6. Turn paper over.

7. Diagonally mountain crease tip of one side over onto itself to create the head. Crease. Your crane is now complete.

The steps of making the crane will look something like this:

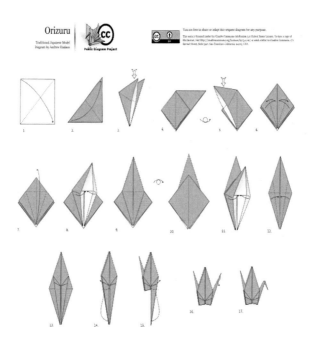

("Tsuri" by Origamidesigner, CC-BY-3.0.)

Along with being a symbol of good fortune, some also believe that if you make 1,000 cranes you'll be granted a wish. While that may not be true, making 1,000 cranes will make you wish that you knew other sculpture patterns to make because you will have definitely honed your origami skills. Yet, you don't have to make 1,000 cranes to perfect your origami skills. If you practice your way through the figures in this book several times, including the crane, you will be ready to tackle other origami figures using the traditional bases. And once again, you'll be able to do it without using a diagram. The following two figures have been provided without diagrams to help you test this mastery.

Traditional Origami Lily

The lily flower symbolizes purity and beauty, and so does the origami lily. This origami sculpture can be used to decorate a centerpiece, or it can be used to add some elegance to gift wrapping.

To make the lily:

1. Make a water bomb base.

2. Squash fold the upper layer of paper.

3. Squash fold the other 3 layers. Your paper should now look like an upside down kite.

4. Rotate paper so that it looks like a right-side-up kite.

5. Valley fold vertically in half, bringing bottom tip to meet top tip. Unfold.

6. Diagonally mountain fold upper edges to center.

Unfold.

7. Squash fold the pocket that has been created in the upper center of the paper on the first layer. To do this, pull down the pocket while refolding the edges. This will create a small flap.

8. Valley fold the flap upwards.

9. Do the same to the other flaps. You should have four flaps.

10. Horizontally valley fold the upper layer of the left flap to the right. Your paper should now look like an elongated diamond.

11. Valley fold lower side edges of the top layer to the center.

12. Do the same for the other three layers.

13. Mountain fold upper tips of each layer so that they are perpendicular to the rest of the paper. You should have six layers to fold like this. This creates the pedals of your lily.

14. You now have an origami lily.

The Butterfly
This origami butterfly is as majestic as a living butterfly. By using colorfully patterned paper, you

can create origami butterflies that are as beautiful as the live ones.

To make the butterfly:

1. Make a pre-crease by making a valley fold and unfolding. Then, make another pre-crease by mountain folding and unfolding. You should have a cross pre-crease.

2. Mountain fold paper in half diagonally, meeting top left corner with bottom right corner. Do the same fold with the top right corner meeting bottom left corner. You should have an X pre-crease.

3. With the paper shaped like a diamond, valley fold in half. You should now have a triangle.

4. Holding bottom corners, push sides in until triangle collapses onto itself. Crease all edges.

5. Valley fold bottom corners of the top layer to meet top corner.

6. Turn over.

7. Repeat Steps 5 and 6 for all layers.

8. Turn over one more time.

9. Unfold top layer while squash folding sides

down. This creates the bottom portion of the wings.

10. Turn the paper over.

11. Mountain fold top point down toward you. Crease.

12. Pleat fold top point back toward top edge of paper using valley fold.

13. Horizontally valley fold in half. Crease.

14. Valley fold bottom right edge to center. Unfold.

15. Do the same for bottom left edge.

16. Turn your paper over.

17. Repeat Steps 13-15. Unfold. Your butterfly is now complete.

The Horse

Here's one last sculpture for you to make. The traditional origami horse makes use of the bird base and the reverse inside fold. There are quite a few steps, but they are simple. Follow the directions carefully, and your sculpture will look ready to be placed on a stand for viewing. Making the horse does require scissors to make a couple of cuts. This just makes the horse easier to fold.

To make the horse:

1. Make a bird base.

2. Squash fold the pocket made by the upper layer. Your paper should look like a diamond with a triangle sticking up behind it (sort of looks like a witches hat).

3. Turn the paper over and do the same to the upper layer. Your paper should now look like a diamond.

4. Cut the paper in the center to the top pre-crease.

5. Valley fold the flaps of the top layer.

6. Mountain fold down (towards you) the tips of the two flaps you just folded. The tops of the flaps should now have a straight edge.

7. Diagonally valley fold the side edges of the paper towards the center. Crease.

8. Turn the paper over.

9. Repeat Steps 4-7. Your paper should now look like a simple figure with his arms raised.

10. Rotate your paper 180 degrees so that the two points are now on the bottom.

11. Mountain fold upper right side of paper so that it's perpendicular to the rest of the paper. Unfold.

12. Make an inside reverse fold to upper right side of the paper.

13. Mountain fold toward you the top corner of the upper left side flap. Unfold.

14. Make an outside reverse fold on the top corner of the upper left side flap. Your horse is now complete.

Final Thoughts

At the beginning of this book, you started with a simple sheet of paper. You then folded your way through simple folds. As you did so, you familiarized yourself with their names and shapes. Moving from there, you created traditional origami bases. After that, you made simple origami models. Then finally, you made some more challenging origami sculptures.

Not only have you progressed through a how-to book on origami, you have also made a progression through your origami skills. In the beginning, you were still unsure of your folds. Now, you can fold with confidence. You started off as a novice, and now you're on your way to becoming an expert.

It's not enough to know just these patterns that you've learned from this book. You should continue on with your origami craft. There are many more models to learn. There's literally a whole world of origami. You could even make an origami world and populate it with origami people and animals. The patterns that you just learned are just the beginning. Seek out new sculptures to make.

Show Your Creativity

Even better, exhibit your creativity by creating your own origami patterns. As you practice your origami skills, your imagination will spring into action. You'll start to envision other shapes that you can make from different combinations of folds. You'll start to see origami shapes in objects around you. Let this creative insight inspire you to create your own patterns. The only limit to your origami collection is your own creative imagination.

Don't Stop Practicing

Now that you have a hobby, now that you've mastered a craft, keep practicing that craft. Enjoy your hobby. When you have spare time, make a model. When you need decorations, make a sculpture. When you simply want to have fun, practice your origami. The point is that you should practice origami whenever you can and as often as you can. Life does get hectic, but creating an origami figure doesn't take long. Origami provides you with a quick break that allows you to relax and refocus.

Relax and Have Fun

The whole point of origami is for you to enjoy the craft. Don't fret over the mistakes. You will make them. You can always start over. Take your time.

Make your folds neatly. Being able to create a figure from a simple piece of paper what makes origami magical. Experience that magic and let it wash away all of the stressors in your life. Origami is a great way to momentarily escape the pressures of life, and that moment is what you need to be able to return to those stressors and overcome them to lead a successful life.

Share Your Hobby

Once you built up enough knowledge to build numerous sculptures, share that knowledge with others. Origami is best when shared. Teach it to your family. Origami can be a great activity over which your family can bond.

Share origami with your friends. If you're friends don't take to origami, find friends that do. Start an origami club in your neighborhood. Ask the local library if you can teach origami to kids during the summer. This is an excellent way of providing the children of your neighborhood a safe, enjoyable activity that enriches their education. It's also a great way to give back to your community.

You could also approach the local hospital about volunteering to teach origami to patients in the hospital. Origami is excellent for making use of the time that patients need to heal. It can also help the patients by taking their minds of their illness. Origami is very therapeutic.

There are so many different ways that you can share origami with others. You don't have to limit yourself to one particular suggestion. You don't even have to follow these suggestions. You can come up with your own way to share origami.

The Versatility of Origami

That is what's so great about origami: its versatility. As an art form, origami is not limited in its form or function. There are many different patterns for creating the same figure. You can choose a simple pattern or a more elaborate pattern depending on your skill level or tastes.

You choose what paper you want to use. You can use a simple color or an intricate design. You can even use plain white copy paper. You can even experiment and make the same model using different papers until you find the one that looks best to you.

In addition to choosing the paper and pattern, you choose when and where you practice paper folding. You don't need a special area to fold paper unlike other crafts. You don't need an origami studio. You may want to keep your paper supplies in a special place so that it doesn't get ruined, but other than that, where you origami is your choice.

Why Not Origami?

With so much to offer, the only choice left for you to make is the choice to continue with paper folding. Make that choice. Choose to make origami a regular part of your life. It's well worth it.

With that being said, enjoy your origami.

Preview of "ONE DAY BEADING MASTERY" by Ellen Warren

Amazon   Link:
**http://www.amazon.com/gp/product/B0
0YB6PSH4**

Introduction - The Amazing world of Bead Making!!

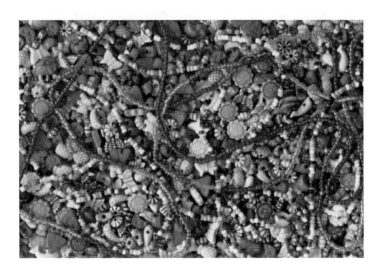

1 Photo by Piyachok Thawornmat

There are many different kinds of jewelry, but one of the richest and most complex types is made from beads. Beads and beaded jewelry can be found in nearly all cultures with many dating back hundreds to thousands of years. Beads can be made of clay, glass, stone, paper, wood, plastic, and metal. They can be found in hundreds of shades and colors, as well as countless shapes and sizes. They can be expensive or cost just pennies a piece, making them accessible for nearly anyone who wants to start creating their own jewelry.

Beading and creating beaded jewelry is a great way of expressing yourself, creating your own personal style, and exercising your creativity. Whether you create something simple or complex, the very art of choosing colors and materials, determining placement, and stringing the beads can unlock your inner artist and personal stylist.

There are a lot of different ways you can use beads to create jewelry. From wire wrapping to coralling, beads can be transformed into rings, bracelets, earrings, and necklace of any style, shape, or personal type of expression. These techniques can be used with beads of nearly any size and shape, from selecting a single color and size of bead to weaving together a variety of different beads made from a mixture of stone, glass, and shell.

So whether you're new to beads and creating beaded jewelry, or you've been experimenting with your own style for some time and are ready for more difficult techniques, learning to work with beads can be a fun and creative way to add some color, texture, and style to your life.

In this book you'll learn the basics of beading from selecting your materials to mixing colors and arranging your layout. You'll also learn some simple tricks for making your own beads out of paper, wood, and clay, and some more intermediate beading techniques to start challenging yourself with.

Beading can be as simple or as complex as you want it to be, making it the ideal medium for people of all levels of artistic expression. Whether you intend to make jewelry for yourself, as a gift, or to start your own craft business, learning to bead can open up a world of different possibilities for you.

Types of Beading

There are a lot of different ways that beads have been used to create various forms of jewelry and decoration. Beads can be strung, woven, or sewed, and there are several different techniques to achieve a variety of different effects.

- The most common type of beadwork is known as threading. This is the act of stringing beads one at a time onto a single strand of thread, wire, or nylon. You can get a lot of different effects using this one simple technique either by varying the beads, varying the length of the thread, or by combining multiple threads together, twisting the strands, or layering them.
- Coralling is type of threading that uses beads to create multiple branches combing off of a single row of beads. Think of the way that a

piece of coral may branch in different directions. So using coralling, you can creating a necklace with several small offshoots or a set of earrings that move in various ways.

- Stitching is one of the more elaborate and complicated methods of beading. There are several different stitches including ladder stitches, brick stitches, peyote stitches, and spiral stitches. Most stitching techniques rely on seed beads or other types of very small beads so you can weave them together to form things like flowers made entirely out of beads.

- Loom beading is a method of weaving threads or stitches through a set of beads to create a sheet of beads. Bags, tassels, and any kind of jewelry meant to drape on the wearer is using woven using this type of technique. Unlike other types of beading, which don't need special equipment beyond the beads, thread, and possibly a needle, loom beading does require both a set pattern and a beading loom to create the desired effects.

Most people when setting out to start making beaded jewelry begin with threading. This technique is so simple that it allows you to work on things like color, texture, and design without worrying about the intricacies of stitches or the type of thread you are using at the same time. You may want to start working with beads in a variety of different patterns at first until you become comfortable with the various effects you can create. After a while, you can begin branching into different stitches to create intricate pendan0ts, broaches, and earrings.

Layouts and Planning

3 Photo by Stuart Miles

No matter what you plan on making, or what technique you'll eventually use, every design begins

78

with the layout. This is the method of arranging your beads in the same order or pattern that you'll eventually use to create the finished piece of jewelry. When you're working with a lot of beads at once, it's helpful to plan while the beads are still loose. Otherwise you can easily find yourself in a position of having a piece that isn't balanced, or that breaks pattern somewhere along the way. Your only recourse at this point in time is usually to start over, so a proper layout can save you a lot of time and frustration latter on.

Plastic trays are available that have narrow channels cut into them just for this purpose. It allows you to arrange your beads in the order you want them without worrying about them rolling away. You can adjust your tray size for the size of the piece that you're working on, and if you're creating a set pattern, you can start it in the tray to ensure that it will work for you before you start threading, without needing to lay out the entire thing.

Spacing

When you're taking the time to lay out your necklace, bracelet, or earrings, make sure you give some thought to the spacing of the beads at the same time. Spaces within a set of beads help the pattern come alive by giving the eye a chance to break apart of the larger sections. They aren't necessary; if you're creating a necklace made up of random beads or a bracelet made of all the same bead then spaces won't need to be part of the design. For other types of jewelry, however, spaces can add a lot of dimension and interest to the design.

Spaces can be achieved in your work in a few different ways:

- Using smaller, plain beads – sometimes known as spacers - between larger patterned ones to break them apart
- Using jump rings between beads to separate them and add dimension to the piece
- Using crimp beads along your wire or thread to stop a bead from sliding and leaving empty space on either side of a larger bead

Depending on the look you want to create, you should take the time to play around with the spacing. If you're using plain beads between patterned ones, consider using different sizes. You can also use varying sizes of the same bead to get similar effects.

Spacing is also a great way to get multiple looks out of

one set of beads. For example, you could make a bracelet with patterned beads broken by plain beads of the same size. Then you could create a second bracelet using the same patterned beads broken by plain beads of a much smaller size. You could even go on to make a bracelet using the same patterned beads but with spaces left by links or empty spaces.

By playing around with these different looks during your layout, you can find the one that works best for the look that you're trying to achieve.

Color and Pattern

You will also want to take color and pattern into consideration when you plan your layout. Jewelry doesn't have to coordinate or even contain multiple shades of the same color, but may designs rely on a mixture of just two or three colors to get the desired look.

Some tips to help you blend things perfectly include:

- Pick up an accent color from within a patterned bead and select some plain beads in this color to intersperse. This will help break up the design and keep the patterned beads from overwhelming the piece.

- Introduce some neutral colors like white, black, gray, or brown to your piece. For example, if the jewelry you are working on seems too dark or looks all of the same color, adding some white can lighten it up dramatically. Likewise, using brown or black in a lighter colored piece can add gravity and interest to the design.

- Consider the color wheel. There are several different ways you can coordinate colors by looking at the color wheel. Complementary colors sit across from one another – think red and green – and they create the most dramatic looks. Analogous colors sit beside each other on the color wheel, and they create more subtle looks, allowing you to blend multiple colors.

- Pay attention to the tone and saturation of the colors you are using. You can combine several different colors and shades as long as your saturation levels – how deep the colors are – remain the same.

When it's time to start arranging the colors, start with the simplest patterns; alternating colors or using a simple A-A-B pattern can give you a good place to start. If you're using a lot of different colors and textures of beads, don't be afraid to use a random pattern either, grabbing whichever bead comes to hand quickest. While you may end up with a run of three of the same color in a row, the overall effect can be striking.

Materials and Things You'll Need

Beads and beading materials come in so many different forms, you may want to experiment with several to discover what type you like best. Not only do beads themselves vary tremendously in terms of color, pattern, size, shape, and material, but the materials you can use to thread them can also vary. Different types of beads also sit differently within a pattern, as well as move differently, while your different threading materials can also give you different end results even when using the same type and pattern of beads.

Therefore, it's important to consider your materials and how they will affect your end project before you begin.

Color and Bead Strings

While there are many specialty stores that sell beads individually, it's a lot easier – and cheaper – to purchase beads by the string. Many beads including glass, stone, ceramic, and metal will be sold strung together on a piece of nylon. Buying your beads this way is a nice way to see how the beads sit next to one another; round beads will sit very differently on a string than chips will, for example.

Some strings will also come with a variety of variegated colors mixed together. If you're unsure about putting colors together, this can be an easy route to take. Otherwise, consider laying out whole strings of beads beside one another in the store to start picking out the perfect colors for your design. Don't be afraid to select multiple beads of the same color as well, changing only things like texture or material to give your finished piece depth.

Irregular and Regular Beads

Beads come in multiple sizes and shapes as well as colors and materials. The biggest difference you'll notice, however, is in the beads' regularity. Stone bead chips, shell beads, and some glass beads will come in varying sizes and shapes within one group or strand. These irregular beads won't function the same way "regular" beads will, beads that have been machined to be uniform in size and shape.

Irregular beads can give you some very interesting looks, however, by giving you a randomness to the jewelry, even when using one bead or color. They can also be the perfect fit in some types of stitching or loom beading; an irregular bead may fit the corner or turn of a piece better than a round or oblong bead might.

Projects made with irregular beads tend to look a little more organic than those made with more uniform beads. So for those that prefer a more "natural" look, these beads might help you achieve the look you're after.

Wire

Many people prefer the use of thread, silk, or cord for beading, but you can get a lot of different looks by using wire. There are three basic types of wire: memory wire, which is difficult to shape, but retains that shape once you achieve it, standard wire which will bend more easily, but unbends easily as well, and woven wire, which acts like a cord, but with a metallic sheen. This type of wire works best for pieces where the thread is visible between the beads.

The key with working with wire is the gauge. Each gauge, or weight of the wire is assigned a number; the higher the number, the thinner and more pliable the wire. Look for 24 gauge wire for delicate wire wrapping or for creating multiple "strands" on a pair of earrings, or for 18 gauge wire to form a coil bracelet.

Jump Rings
Jump rings are fully formed circles of wire that are not easily unbent. You can join a bunch of them together to form a chain, hang several strands of beads off one ring, or use them as spacers between beads. You can usually find jump rings in two types: the first will require pliers to bend open and then shut again, while the second works more like a miniature key chain that you twist to attach to another.

Pliers
You will want at least two pairs of pliers when working

with beaded jewelry. One pair should have a flat nose, while the other should be rounded. Ideally, they should also be two different sizes to give you some more flexibility in this area. You'll need the pliers to hold small beads as you thread them, open jump rings, bend the end of a wire into a loop, or to close a crimp bead.

Beading Needle and Thread

If you plan on using actual thread for your beads, rather than cord or wire, you should invest in a beading needle as well. Beading needles are thin, flexible pieces of metal with a large eye. To use them, you tie the end of your piece of thread to the needle, then use the needle to string multiple beads at a time onto your thread. Most of the time, you'll use a beading needle with thin cotton or silk thread. This is ideal for coralling, stitching, or any type of beading where you want to double back through a bead or around the outside of a bead.

Making Your Own Beads

In addition to the beads that you can find in craft stores, bead stores, and specialty shops, there are also numerous types of beads that are easy to make yourself.

Making your own beads has a lot of advantages for jewelry makers:

- It's low cost, perfect for those who are on a budget, or who make a lot of jewelry
- It allows you to create unique and one of a kind pieces that may be unlike anything else that could be found in a store

- It gives you greater control over the project as whole; if you are unable to find beads that match your vision, you may be able to create those beads yourself to get the perfect finished look for your piece

Beads can be made out of nearly any material. Remember, that long before there were the types of mass-machined beads being sold today, that cultures and people where creating their own beads out a variety of different materials.

Wood Beads
Add a very lightweight, rustic, and often colorful touch to your jewelry with wooden beads. Making wooden beads is extremely simple, and can be done with objects you find in and around your home.

What you need:

- Several branches or sticks ranging in thickness from 1/8 inch to ½ inch
- Metal or wood trimmers
- Drill with a 1/16 inch bit
- Paint of your choosing

What to do:

1. Cut the branches or sticks into pieces ranging from ½ to 1 inch in length
2. Peel the bark from some of the pieces – you may want experiment with leaving the bark on some of your beads for additional texture
3. Drill vertically down the center of each piece of wood
4. Paint the exterior of the beads

Wooden beads are very light and easy to work with. You can mix them with other materials for a very unique and personal piece.

Shell Beads

If you live near the beach, you can make your own beads right out of the shells you find there. This technique works not only for small, whole shells but for those numerous tiny shell pieces that are often found all over the water's edge. Shell beads can add a lot of dimension, and mixed with things like glass and stone can make some beautiful vacation-style necklaces.

What you need:

- Shells or shell fragments of all sizes
- Diamond or carbide-tipped drill bit of about 1/16-inch in size
- Cooling oil

- Pliers
- Piece of wood block

What to do:

1. Grasp the piece of shell or shell fragment between the pliers.
2. Dip the end of the drill bit into the cooling oil.
3. Hold the piece of shell firmly against the wood block so the part you are drilling is in contact with the wood.
4. Set your drill to a high speed and drill quickly straight down through the shell until it reaches the wood belong.

[Excerpts from the first 3 Chapters – for complete book, please purchase on Amazon.com]

Made in United States
North Haven, CT
31 May 2023

37197853R00052